WORDS ABOUT WIZARDS

ALSO BY ROBERT PARRISH

You'd Be Surprised (with John Goodrum)
Do That Again (with Oscar Weigle)
For Magicians Only
New Ways to Mystify
Inside Magic (with George Boston)
My Uncle and Miss Elizabeth (novel)
52 Amazing Card Tricks (for Rufus Steele)
Paul Rosini's Magical Gems (for Rufus Steele)
The Last Word on Cards (for Rufus Steele)
Okito on Magic (with Theodore Bamberg)
Six Tricks by Tenkai
Bert Allerton's The Close-Up Magician
An Evening with Charlie Miller
Parrish Folio (*The Pallbearers Review*, Summer 1974)
Illusion Show, by David Bamberg (Editor)

*Recollections of magicians
and their magic, 1930-1950*

 # Words About Wizards

Robert Parrish

David Meyer ✳ Magic Books
Glenwood, Illinois
1994

Copyright © 1994 by Robert Parrish
All rights reserved. This book, or parts thereof,
may not be reproduced in any form or by any means
without written permission from the publisher.
ISBN 0-916638-79-0

Library of Congress Cataloging–in–Publication Data

Parrish, Robert, 1918–
   Words about wizards / Robert Parrish.
     p. cm.
   Includes index.
   ISBN 0–916638–79–0 :
   1. Magicians—United States.   I. Title.
GV1545.A2P37   1994
793.8'092'2—dc20
[B]   94–4293
                                                                               CIP

David Meyer ✻ Magic Books
is an imprint of
Meyerbooks, Publisher
P.O. Box 427
Glenwood, Illinois 60425

Contents

Introduction
ix

Words About Wizards
1

Some American Magicians of the 1930s
19

Who Was Rufus Steele?
46

Index
53

Illustrations

George Boston taking a card from Harry Blackstone at Society of American Magicians convention, Chicago, 1947	3
The Blackstone show in performance at the Erlanger Theatre, Chicago, 1950	4
Okito in Oriental makeup, Berlin, probably mid-1920s	5
Charlie Miller performing the Egg Bag, Chicago, July, 1959	8
Harlan Tarbell Testimonial, Chicago, November 24, 1956	10
John Mulholland	14
Ricardo Richardine, Theo Bamberg, Marga, Ricardo, Jr., at the Senate Theatre, Chicago, 1957	16
Jack Gwynne in 1929 theatrical poses	20
Ed Reno in his later years	25
Joseffy, circa 1910	30
Balsamo	31
Paul Rosini	33
Mysterious Smith	36
Ade Duval, 1934	40
Paul LePaul springing the cards into the hat	42
LePaul early in his career	43
W. F. (Rufus) Steele	47

Acknowledgments

I wish to thank Donald Bevan, editor of *Abracadabra,* and Davenports, owners of that magazine, and the New England Magic Collectors Association and Ed Hill and Bob Schoof, editors of *The Yankee Magic Collector,* for permission to reprint articles that first appeared in their periodicals.

Appreciation is also due to Anita Meyer for expertly typing the final draft, to my wife, Mary, for tireless proofreading and for editorial advice, and to David Meyer for being a publisher who cares deeply about his products.

Introduction

This collection of sketches about magicians who figured in the first half of the present century came about by accident. It had to do with my giving a talk before a group of bibliophiles about magicians I had known and admired and, in some cases, for whom I had served as a scribe. At the behest of Jay Marshall, I repeated the performance at a magic convention, then forgot about the whole thing.

There were several requests for copies of the speech, but I was unable to find the manuscript in my chaotic files. Finally I initiated a more intensive search and, in the course of doing so, found other drafts, including a series of articles on American magicians of the 1930s written in 1967 for the British magazine *Abracadabra,* and an article on Rufus Steele, which I contributed to *The Yankee Magic Collector #3,* 1988. It occurred to me that if these scattered pieces were brought together, they might form a document of some current interest and future usefulness.

Anecdotes about magicians of the past and descriptions of their performances have always held great fascination for me. Here are notes on some remarkable people who flourished 40 or more years ago.

 # Words About Wizards

The two interests which have led me to accumulate large numbers of books are English literature and magic.

I think my interest in magic is congenital. There is an inborn obliquity of vision that seems to be shared by most magicians—a way of looking at the world and finding something there quite other than what you would expect. However, my interest in magic as a craft dates from the seventh grade (that would be about 60 years ago) when I first saw a professional magician, and a good one at that, Gerald Heany. I knew then and there that magic was for me and headed for the library to learn more about it. And the public library in Mason City, Iowa, turned out to be the right place. They had a fine collection of classic magic books.

One of the delights of English literature—and especially that of the first half of the present century—is that everyone writing knew everyone else and everyone kept diaries and wrote memoirs and countless letters, and published them. The result is an endless store of anecdotes through which these people come alive. There is even an *Oxford Book of Literary Anecdotes,* and it just scratches the surface.

Presented at the May 3, 1991 luncheon meeting of The Caxton Club, Chicago.

Now, magic—and you understand I'm talking about stage magic, conjuring, entertaining deception—has an astonishingly large literature, mostly technical, mostly privately published for limited circulation. There is also a good deal of historical material, and this became my special interest because I found the people in magic even more fascinating than the illusions they perpetrated.

When I got out of the army in 1946 and settled in Chicago, I encountered a man who knew magic, who had a fund of anecdotes revealing the curiosities of character among magical showmen, and who possessed a dramatic flair for making these anecdotes come alive. His name was George Boston. He had worked as an assistant for some of the top stage magicians and had been fired by all of them. This wasn't due to incompetence. George was a superb assistant and he knew stagecraft. But he was a classic manic-depressive. It went with his dramatic flair. Anyway, we wrote a book called *Inside Magic* that later provided George with an entree to Hollywood, where his temperament seemed much less bizarre than it did in Chicago. He spent the rest of his working life as a technical consultant and background person in motion pictures and television.

As the guy who did the writing, I began to get requests for literary help from magicians whom I admired very much and whose lives and times I should have been very interested in recording. As it turned out, this was not as easy as it seemed.

One of the first to approach me was a man whom I regarded as the outstanding American stage magician of the period, Harry Blackstone, Sr. Blackstone wanted an autobiography, so I went up to Milwaukee where he was opening his season at the Davidson Theatre (a legitimate house, now long gone) to talk it over. What I discovered about Blackstone was something I have found to be common to many showmen. He

George Boston taking a card from Harry Blackstone at Society of American Magicians convention, Chicago, 1947

had devoted his life to creating a persona—the creation that enchanted his audiences and that made him a great magician. He really wasn't interested in the man, Harry Boughton, born in very modest circumstances on the South Side of Chicago in 1885, or in the struggles that went into creating a great magic show and keeping it on the road for over forty years. What he wanted was a romance, an invention commensurate with his invention of Blackstone the Magician, and I was neither competent to do this nor interested in doing so.

The Blackstone show in performance at the Erlanger Theatre, Chicago, 1950

The next great magician who wanted me to write a book for him was a retired Dutch conjurer named Theodore Bamberg, who was the most artistic performer of magic I have ever witnessed. He was the fifth or possibly the sixth generation in a consecutive line of magicians to the crown of Holland. In the guise of an Oriental magician named Okito, he presented an act which headlined in virtually every great variety theatre in Europe in the 1920s and 1930s. In addition to his superb theatrical deportment and skill as a magician, he was a great craftsman and an originator of many fine magical illusions. I was delighted to work with him on a book called *Okito on Magic*, which was published in 1952 and is still in print.

Okito in Oriental makeup, Berlin, probably mid-1920s

The book is largely concerned with Okito's technical contributions to magic, but about 50 pages are devoted to his memoirs. Here again, I found it very difficult to get Okito to talk about Theodore Bamberg. The subject of his life was illusion, and what actually happened didn't make much difference. He was quite brilliant in his recollections of other magicians of the first half of the century. But when I asked for anecdotes related to his own life, he would come up with fabrications, some of them quite ingenious.

After Theo Bamberg's death in 1963 at the age of 88, I corresponded with his son, David, who was South America's greatest magician. David wrote: "To tell you the truth, I was rather disappointed when I read his book. I can't understand why he didn't 'give' to you and tell you the real story. . . . Maybe a false pride prevented him from going deeply into matters, but do you know that after his brilliant [early] success in Europe, he came to America in 1908 and shortly after sold the act. . . . Then followed a period when he was at a loose end and tried opening a magic store, traveling with Thurston, combining with Zancig [the mentalist], until finally he tried to commit suicide in Brooklyn by poisoning. Finally, he pulled himself together and went to South America where he started all over again and in a short time had the most beautiful and original act of his whole career and was the rage of Europe. At one time he was head and shoulders over all the other magicians in Europe, with a salary of a thousand gold marks a day in the Scala-Berlin. And this was for a 20 minute act—not a full night's show. . . . It was one of the greatest comebacks in the history of magic."

During my acquaintance with Okito, he pointed out to me that unlike many magical showmen, he never used the term "great magician" in his publicity. In fact, he said, the posters advertising his appearances simply bore the name Okito. This was quite true and I was properly impressed. After his death, I inherited some of his personal effects, including a small casket containing fine woodworking tools. On the inside of the lid of the casket, visible only to Okito while he was engaged in crafting his apparatus, was a plaque which read: "Okito, the Greatest Oriental Magician the World Has Ever Known."

In the time that remains, I should like to tell you about a man who was born obsolete, a magician who really believed in magic, the dilemma of a children's entertainer, and the secret of success of a traveling showman.

Charlie Miller

Charles Earle Miller (1909-1989) was born obsolete. His father was a successful piano manufacturer in Indianapolis. The family was well off and Charlie was educated by a private tutor. When Charlie became interested in a subject, he pursued it relentlessly, and one of these subjects was sleight of hand. By the time he was 20, he was recognized by people in the profession as one of the great sleight-of-hand men in the country. He devoted himself to the performance of classical drawing room effects. These are the greatest magical effects ever originated. They are the products of the genius of certain 19th century European magicians who performed primarily in the private drawing rooms of great houses and who refined the art of magic to meet the requirements of this discriminating audience. Chamber music was written for the same circumstances. Drawing room conjuring is the chamber music of magic.

Charlie Miller had more than just the skill to perform classical magic. He was built for it. He was a fat man, and a fat man causes us both to smile and to drop our guard. He also had the innate grace common to rotund people—probably in order to keep their balance. He was the most delightful, most skilled, most mystifying of performers. The only problem was that the field for which his art was designed no longer existed. He was born 100 years too late.

The great houses were gone, but Charlie was known—

Charlie Miller performing the Egg Bag, Chicago, July, 1959

indeed, he was somewhat legendary—among persons with a deep interest in magic and he was often invited to their homes. His family fortunes had declined and he ultimately became a perpetual house guest. In fact, he resided at my house for about three months. During this time, he remained practically invisible, and for a 300-pound man, that's quite a trick. I even wrote a little book for him, and that's still in print, too. But the day came when Charlie finally said to me, "Bob, I've made a decision. This has got to stop. I'm going to quit being a guest of society. I'm going to get a job. My father taught me a skill that very few people know anything about. I know how to make ivory piano keys. I have an appointment to see someone tomorrow at the Kimball Piano Company, and I think they'll hire me."

"Charlie," I said, "I think that's a wonderful plan."

The next day, Charlie dressed neatly for his appointment and my wife and I gave him a big breakfast and sent him off. "Good luck, Charlie!"

It was a hot summer day in Chicago and Charlie was a bit wilted when he returned. We sat him down and gave him a drink. "Tell us all about it."

"Well," Charlie said, "they were very interested in my background. In fact, the personnel manager called in several of the executives and they seemed fascinated. The only problem is, very few pianos today have ivory keys. The keys are made of plastic for all but the most expensive models. So one old man in Indiana now makes all the ivory piano keys for all the piano manufacturers in America."

This story has a happy ending. Some time later, two young men in California, the Larsen brothers, refurbished an old mansion and created a private club which they called The Magic Castle. It provided ideal performing conditions for Charlie Miller's kind of magic. So Charlie was able to spend his declining years basking in the Southern California sun and in the applause of an admiring public.

The moral is: The best thing in the world is to be an obsolete man whose time has come.

Harlan Tarbell

Harlan Tarbell (1890-1960) was an all-American nut. He was a Roycrofter, a disciple of Elbert Hubbard, who founded an arts and crafts colony in the pattern of William Morris. Tarbell once explained to me the Roycrofter philosophy. If a Roycrofter wanted to write a book, he should first cut down a tree and

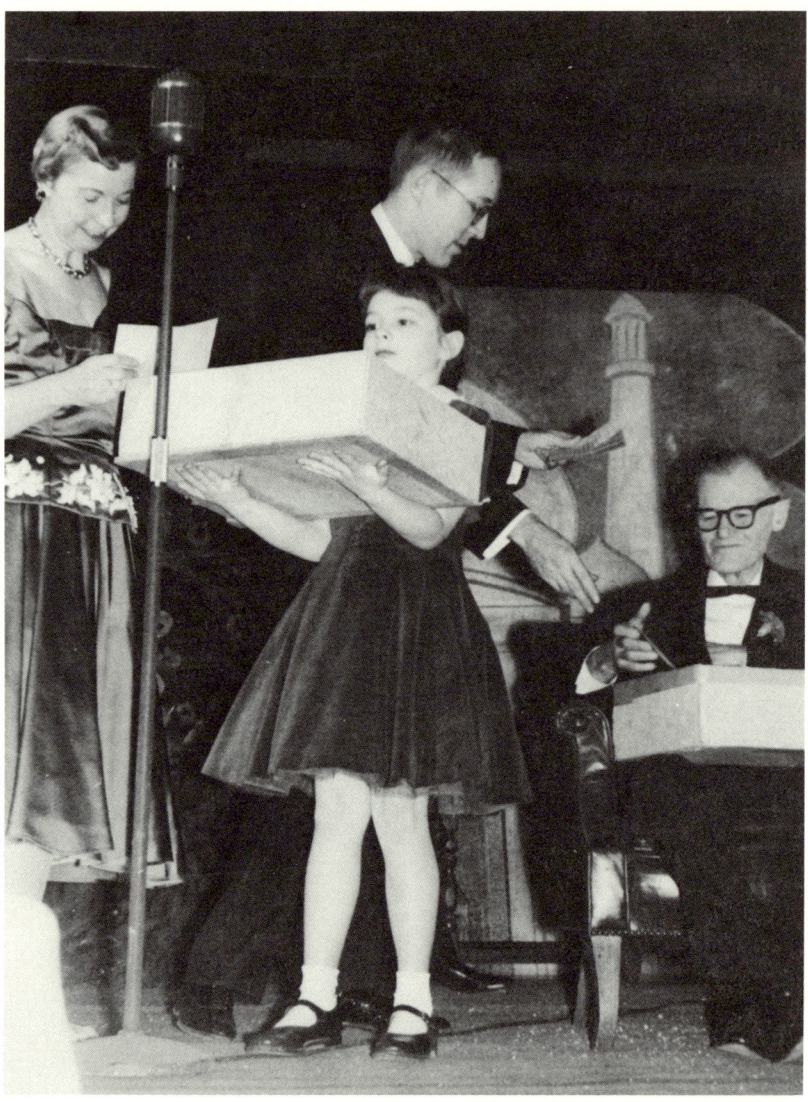

Harlan Tarbell Testimonial, Chicago, November 24, 1956. Left to right: Frances Marshall reading letters of appreciation, Mary Parrish holding box of letters, Robert Parrish handing messages to Tarbell.

make paper from the pulp, then go on from there through typesetting, printing, and binding. Tarbell was also a vegetarian, a napropath (everyone called him Doc), a Mason, a theosophist, and probably a Rotarian.

Tarbell was a magician who believed in magic. Almost half a century ago, he wrote a guest editorial in a magic journal. In it he said: "One of my great pleasures in life has been the knowing and talking in confidence with many of the world's truly great Magicians. Not only our magicians of the stage, but those grand Magicians—those Magi of the Inner Brotherhoods whose knowledge of life is so far beyond the age in which we live."

To Tarbell, everything in magic or in nature pointed to something beyond itself. Everything was a metaphor.

During the late 1920s, Tarbell wrote and illustrated a superb correspondence course in magic. But his first book was not a magic book. It was a book on chalk talk published in 1920. He then wrote a book, published in 1923, called *Here's Power, Read Character Instantly, A Magic Key to People's Minds*, by Harlan E. Tarbell and John B. Rolle—Based on the Metaphor System. Quoting the dust jacket: "Don't Guess What People Are—KNOW!"

I have met believers in the occult whom I have found merely irritating, people who it seemed to me had abandoned the world in which we live for a world of fantasy. This was never the case with Harlan Tarbell. He was a tough, realistic showman and a folksy, humorous Middle Western American. To the greeting, "How are you?" he might respond, "Eh? I'm just a young feller trying to get along."

To Tarbell there *was* no distinction between the natural and the supernatural. He walked across the dividing line between them without noting any difference. It was all the same to him and accepted in the same down-to-earth manner.

This made conversation with Tarbell a source of great delight to me. Once, when he came back from a trip to Britain, he gave me an account of a visit to the Isle of Man, where he was the guest of a notable British eccentric named Sir Alexander Cannon, who professed occult powers and maintained a sanatorium to improve the psychic health of his patients.

Tarbell described a treatment at the hands of Sir Alexander. They laid Doc Tarbell on an examination table and Sir Alexander sent his spirit control ten miles above him so she could look straight down through the Doc.

"Oh, Bob," Tarbell said to me, "it's so far ahead of X-Ray." And, he said, "You know there are certain tricks you've seen me do where at a particular point I have a little trouble with them. Well, she traced the cause right back to my Spanish incarnation.

"Oh, Bob," he said, "you can't beat that old Tibetan training."

Magicians had varying opinions about Tarbell's powers as a magical showman. Laymen didn't. They thought he was wonderful. A business acquaintance told me about booking Tarbell for his club's ladies' night. He said that the evening of the show, this thin, bent old man showed up carrying two suitcases and representing himself as Dr. Tarbell. My friend said, "Where's the show?"

Tarbell said, "Eh, eh, eh—right here," and went ahead with borrowing some card tables and some chairs and draping them with various foulards. The curtain went up on a colorful stage setting and Doc Tarbell came out swinging his arms and addressing the audience in his chatty style. My friend said, "It was the best show we ever had."

Harlan Tarbell was an unlikely figure of a magician, but his belief carried over into his show. The tricks were magic in his hands because he knew they were metaphors pointing to the profound and inexpressible.

John Mulholland

Another magician of note was John Mulholland, who for 23 years brilliantly edited the leading journal for magicians, *The Sphinx*. His collection of magical literature was one of the greatest in the world. He died in 1970, leaving the collection to The Players Club in New York City.

John was probably the first professional magician to assume the role of conjurer-lecturer. And with the exception of his shows for children and a few theatrical appearances, this was the role he always played. His success was not the result of physical attributes associated with a man of magic, but of sheer force of intellect. John was a tall man with a large head, a receding chin, a dignified bearing, and a slightly hesitant mode of speech. Yet he had warm charm and I found him delightful both as a performer and as a person.

John was born in Chicago in 1898 and there is some evidence that eccentricity ran in his family. When John first needed a passport (his mother took him on a trip around the world), he discovered he had no birth certificate. His father had "forgotten" to have the birth recorded. John's mother then went to Chicago from New York to take care of the matter, presenting herself to the proper official and stating that she wished to register a birth.

The official recorded Mrs. Mulholland's name and vital data, then said, "How old is the father?"

"He has been dead many years," Mrs. Mulholland said.

"In that case, how old is the child?"

John Mulholland

"Twenty-six years old," Mrs. Mulholland stated firmly.

A self-possessed man, John recognized his vulnerability to being caught off guard and he told some engaging stories about this happening to him. One such anecdote concerned a children's show.

John had been engaged to perform for a little girl's birthday party. The birthday child and her guests were assembled in an elegantly appointed drawing room. John's program included a version of the Ring in the Nest of Boxes, which he performed very artistically, the borrowed ring ultimately appearing tied to a flower found within a set of nested, locked boxes.

John began by saying, "I should like to borrow some little girl's ring." He was appalled to see the smallest child in the room, a mere toddler, rise to her feet and approach bearing a ring on her outstretched hand. In the course of the trick, the ring would apparently be destroyed and John feared such a little girl might burst into tears. However, there was nothing for it but to go ahead.

"My," he said admiringly as he bent down to her, "is this *your* ring?"

"Yes," said the little girl.

"Such a *pretty* ring," he said, taking it.

"Yes," she said proudly in a small, clear voice.

"Now, I am going to put your ring into the barrel of the magic gun."

"Yes."

"Oh, the ring is too big to go into the barrel."

"Yes."

"I'll just tap it with this little hammer," he said, bringing the hammer down onto the ring with horrifying impact.

"Now *that* was a hell of a thing to do!" she said.

Ricardo Richardine, Sr.

For every magician who has attained widespread recognition in the eyes of the public and of fellow conjurers, there have been many others of great ability who spent lifetimes in show business and yet are virtually unknown. These invisible performers provide an intriguing field for the magical historian. The great

Left to right: Ricardo Richardine, Theo Bamberg, Marga, Ricardo, Jr., at the Senate Theatre, Chicago, 1957

and often sparsely populated spaces of North America have provided a natural field for such performers: for example, Gus Rapp, who spent fifty years in trouping, seldom playing a town large enough to be shown on a map, and the Willard Family, performing for generations under canvas in the virtually unexplored reaches of Texas and Louisiana.

South America also provided a fertile ground for this kind

of truly independent showman. Such a performer was Ricardo Richardine. Richardine, with his son Ricardo, Jr. and his daughter Marga, turned up in Chicago in 1957 at a theatre that played Spanish movies. I had never heard of him. The production was well-staged and spectacular. The equipment was immaculate. Richardine came back for a second engagement.

During both of his Chicago engagements, delegations of Chicago magicians (including Okito) attended the show at his invitation and he added special material for them, such as his superb presentation of the Linking Rings.

At the second engagement, while the Spanish movie was concluding, the local magicians grouped in the lobby around a cage containing a not very contented lion. Ricardo, Sr. joined the group and explained that he had purchased the lion for an illusion, but when his boys tried to handle it, the beast proved intractable. After the show, Richardine joined with the magicians and we had a wonderful conversation, but I did not learn the secret of how this theatrical enterprise had endured and, apparently, prospered.

The following week, the engagement ended and a concluding event, reported in the newspapers, gave me a clue to the secret of Richardine's survival: boundless guile.

What would you do if you were a magician who played Spanish-language theatres and you were stuck with a useless lion?

Ricardo Richardine knew what to do. On the last night, he sold raffle tickets for the lion. This most likely yielded more than the purchase price of the beast. Of course, the winner could scarcely be expected to take his prize home with him, so the magician bought the lion back for $75. Then Richardine sold the lion for something under its original purchase price to Wild Kingdom, the exotic animal house from which it had come. Thus everyone came out ahead: the lucky winner, the animal dealer, and the magician.

Today, theatrical illusions with wild beasts have become something of a vogue, but it was Richardine, Sr. who had the alchemical secret for transmuting base beasts into gold.

 *Some American Magicians of the 1930s*

Jack Gwynne

While the position of vaudeville in American entertainment began to decline after World War I, it continued for another two decades as an adjunct to films in the largest theaters in major cities. During the '30s the number of magicians who regularly played these top houses was extremely limited. Among these performers, Jack Gwynne (1895-1969) was one of the few magicians presenting an act of what we might classify as general magic, in the apparatus and small illusion class.

As the opening act on the bill at the Palace Theatre in Chicago in 1937, Gwynne's performance ran as follows:

1. *Production of Rabbit from a Box.* This effect was typical of Gwynne's approach to apparatus magic. The box consisted of panels lying flat on a tray. It took no explaining to tell you there was nothing there. The panels were so hinged that when lifted they at once formed a box, from which a very large rabbit was quickly produced. The rabbit then made a mighty leap from Gwynne's arms to the box (held by an assistant), providing an effective applause cue.

2. *The Cut and Restored Turban.* The roll of cloth was a long one and its handling provided an attractive visual picture.

Upon restoration, performer and assistants marched forward, again drawing applause.

3. *Rooster Vanish from a Small Box.* As with the rabbit, the rooster was established as a distinct personality, an impor-

Jack Gwynne (twice) in 1929 theatrical poses

tant element in livestock tricks. The handling of this effect was a lesson both in buildup and in misdirection. The rooster was put in the box and a foulard thrown over the whole thing. The foulard was then folded up and handed to Anne Gwynne (Jack's wife), who held it with undue care while the box was disassembled. At the exact instant the gimmicked panel was removed, she shook out the foulard, showing it clearly innocent. The table upon which the box had stood remained. In the process of showing it, a feather protruded, but this proved only to be a duster, completing the sucker effect.

4. *Bowl Productions.* Three large bowls of water were produced from what looked like an Indian carpet and were poised upon three stands which were linked together on a base rolled in on casters. Byplay involving an apparent materialization beneath the carpet which turned out to be the performer's foot heightened interest, created a laugh, and covered the introduction of the taborets.

5. *Silks and Stack of Bowls Production.* From one of the bowls, a large quantity of silks was produced. These were gathered up and held over the stand upon which the original bowl was situated, then lifted to reveal a tall stack of fishbowls. The bowls were quickly unstacked and emptied into a large pail to prove that each, indeed, was separate and full of water. Gwynne stepped forward, wiping his hands, to receive applause for this truly amazing production. The misdirection for stealing the stack of bowls was perfect and defied detection.

6. *Temple of Benares.* This Doll House version of the Sword Cabinet, which has now become a standard effect, was one of Gywnne's most widely imitated originations.

7. *Torn and Restored Magazine Page.* Gwynne closed in one with his showmanly version of this familiar torn and restored effect, with sucker explanation. He offered to show a

piece of pure sleight of hand, with hands completely isolated from the body. For this purpose, he stood behind a banner, suspended from a crossbar, with his hands protruding through two holes in the banner. Tearing of the paper was synchronized with the music.

Gwynne's material was pirated by innumerable performers, but the timing and the perfect coordination on the part of the assistants could not be imitated. He was probably the first to adapt an act of this type to night club floor shows and was fully successful in this field as in vaudeville. He continued to introduce new material, always with an original touch. An example of buildup with a small trick was his version of the Tenkai two-glass suspension employing very tall tumblers and illuminating the suspended glasses for purposes of a walk down into the audience with a flashlight in the sleeve. The Spirit Table was another effect around which Gwynne built a highly effective presentation. Manipulation of the table established its uncanny character prior to its levitation.

After World War II, the Gwynne family built a full-evening show which they played under the auspices of various organizations. It included many large illusions, the most spectacular of which was the evanishment of the entire company from a tent on a high platform. All came running down the aisle from the back of the theatre.

Stowell's Oriental Oddities

A well-produced vaudeville act of the late 1920s and early '30s was Stowell's Oriental Oddities. The performer and two assistants, all in Chinese costume, opened with a series of effects which included the vanishing bowl of water, production of doves and their evanishment from a breakaway box and subsequent reproduction from another box, and a silk production. The silks as produced were held by the two assistants and when gathered together were suddenly transformed into an enormous silk which was held high by the assistants, completely concealing the performer. This silk, which had probably been stolen from the back of one of the assistants, was then dropped, revealing the performer, whose costume was now changed to Occidental full-dress. (This almost instantaneous costume change was used in later years by the Japanese performer Kuma, whose act was built around the traditional Oriental production trick employing two nesting cylinders. In America this trick is known as the Kuma Tubes. After World War II Kuma worked under the name of Kim.)

Stowell now stepped forward and announced that he would present his latest illusion, the Chinese Torture Cabinet. These were the only words spoken during the act.

Curtains opened for full-stage presentation of the slicing a woman into four pieces illusion. The apparatus was purchased from Stowell by McDonald Birch in the mid-'30s; Birch used it for the rest of his career. It consisted of a platform supporting a long box composed of four hinged segments. The female assistant was secured to the top of the platform with restraints at the neck and ankles, then covered with the segmented box. A sword was then driven through each section of the box, from top to bottom. A large, flat-bladed instrument in the nature of a halberd was introduced and passed completely between each segment of the box. Needless to say, the girl emerged unscathed.

Stowell's presentation was outstanding for the speed with which the various actions were performed and the pattern of movement involving both the penetrations and the wheeling of the platform to permit the operations to be seen from various angles in a beautifully regulated and convincing sequence. As performed by Stowell, this was as baffling and effective an illusion as it is possible to imagine.

An important point which I learned from this presentation is that the "convincing" touches in magic need not be overdone. The securing of the girl to the top of the platform was carried out rapidly and without undue emphasis. It simply suggested that the girl could not easily get away. If a committee had come up and locked her into place, the suggestion would have been that she was undoubtedly going to *try* to get free, and the audience would have been set unnecessarily to thinking ahead toward a solution. Here the shock of what occurred followed swiftly and continued to build, defying belief.

The small magic which opened the act, although largely a buildup for the quick-change and the illusion, was executed with quiet perfection. It might have had greater impact, however, if a factor in the layman's thinking had been considered: the solution to each effect performed could well have been attributed to the wide Oriental sleeves of the performer's costume. Yet it so happens that Oriental sleeves can be turned back both easily and gracefully, and the very action of doing so (as anyone who has seen Okito can testify) provides a showmanly buildup for the feat to follow.

Ed Reno

"Uncle Ed" Reno (1861-1949) was one of the best-loved chautauqua entertainers. Chautauqua was the designation for a quasi-educational institution which consisted of lectures, musical and dramatic presentations, and variety acts, presented

Ed Reno in his later years

over a series of days, usually under canvas. It flourished in the smaller communities of America over a period of several decades.

I once worked for a man named Harrington who had been a unit manager for the Redpath Bureau, the largest booking agency in the chautauqua field. One summer Harrington's troupe included Reno and a Northwestern University professor who gave Shakespearean recitations. The magician and the Shakespearean developed a close association, but one day Uncle Ed learned that his friend's weekly paycheck was somewhat larger than his own. He went to Harrington with a strongly worded complaint, the most memorable line of which was: "And you know, that son of a bitch couldn't pull a rabbit out of a hat if his life depended on it!"

Chautauqua performers were prohibited from engaging in money-making sidelines, but Uncle Ed regularly sold a small trick book in the course of his performances. He announced, however, that the entire proceeds went to the "Old Magician's Home" in Kankakee, Illinois. The spectators, of course, did not know that the Reno residence was in Kankakee.

By the 1930s, chautauqua had expired as an institution, but Reno continued to work on the school show circuits. I first saw him while I was in high school in Mason City, Iowa.

Reno was a rather portly old gentleman with a strong, open countenance. He began his show by stating that magic was shortly to be taught in the schools and that each student would be issued a wand along with his books. Unlike today's magician, Reno used the wand constantly, and a recurring line of patter was, "It's all in the stick."

He opened with the Sucker Torn and Restored Napkin, presented as a magic lesson. Then he performed the Vanishing Wand, followed by the Vanishing Cane. The latter was the old European type which telescoped slowly between the hands, followed by the reproduction of a solid cane from the trouser pocket.

Out of a very large repertoire, presented with great authority, the following items seemed outstanding:

1. *Ball Casket and Cage Canister.* A large tin canister was filled with colored balls from a glass-sided box. The balls visibly reappeared in the box. In place of the balls, the canister was found to contain a large cage housing a dove.

2. *Rising Cards.* The cards were placed in a houlette mounted on a long stick which was then impaled on the seat of a wooden chair. Reno and a boy from the audience stood some distance from this contrivance while the selected cards rose. At the conclusion, the boy was asked to remove the pack from the holder. A masterpiece of misdirection and boldness.

3. *Routine of Color Changes with a Pack of Cards.* Finally a single card held at the fingertips changed visibly.

4. *Ink to Water.* The change took place with the boy assistant holding the glass throughout.

5. *Body Loads.* Reno was a master of this seemingly lost art and the quantity of material produced from the clothing of assisting spectators during the course of the performance appeared inexhaustible. Periodic departures from the stage to reload were covered in amusing ways. In one instance, a boy holding a paper cornucopia was warned sternly against peeking inside the cone, but was cued to do so when the performer reached the wings. The resulting hilarity gave Reno ample time to replenish his pockets.

6. *Dove Decapitation.* The head of a dove produced in the course of an effect was apparently twisted off (actually tucked under the wing) and tossed into a girl's lap, where it was found to be a ball of cotton. In questionable taste, but a delight to the schoolboy's heart.

7. *Production of Bowls of Water.* It has always seemed to me technically wrong for a magician to open with productions from the body. Reno used the bowl productions near the end of his performance. He draped a not too large black foulard over his arm and without any fuss produced a shallow glass bowl brimming with water. This bowl was set aside and the performer at once came down the steps into the audience and produced a second bowl.

8. *Borrowed Handkerchief in Nest of Boxes.* One-man method and a profound mystery.

9. *Duck Vanish.* Performed with several boy assistants, standing at either side of the box in which the duck was deposited. The box was then disassembled, the pieces being thrown on the floor with abandon. I had no idea where the duck went.

Several years later, the school principal gave me his story of this particular performance. He had gone down to the stage to meet the magician he had booked and was appalled to encounter an evidently sick old man unpacking the worst-looking junk he had ever seen in the way of stage props. His first thought was to cancel the show, but since the performer professed to be in perfect readiness to go on, the principal resigned himself to disaster. He took the precaution, however, of inventing a new school regulation which required that the principal sit on the stage during all presentations in the auditorium. The magician showed no evidence of concern over this vagary and continued with his preparations. "How did you feel about it when it was all over?" I asked. "It was the greatest show we ever had," the principal said.

In his book *Leaves from Conjurers' Scrap Books,* published in 1891, H.J. Burlingame wrote: "One of the rising young magicians of the present time is Edward Reno. He carries a large, first-class outfit, and is one of the few that knows how to work what he has to advantage. His experience dates from the year 1880. In the manipulation of his tricks and apparatus he shows a skill rarely surpassed. He is noted as one who always gives what is called 'a square show.'"

Forty years later, "Uncle Ed" had lost none of his skill. He still gave a square show.

Joseffy

Josef Freud (1873-1946) was a mechanical genius who performed in chautauqua in the earlier years of the century under the name of Joseffy. His show consisted of his own inventions, which are reported to have amazed magicians and laymen alike. He later became a successful electrical engineer, highly regarded for his ability to solve difficult technical problems. During the 1930s he occasionally appeared on shows staged by Chicago magical organizations, presenting his best-known origination, the Skull of Balsamo.

As a stage personality, Joseffy was enormously impressive—hawk-faced, mustachioed, and with a wild shock of white hair. His deep voice completed the image of a personage quite capable of dealing in the supernatural.

I was somewhat taken aback when this legendary creator of the mechanically marvelous opened his act by doing a trick with a stacked deck. After having several spectators remove clusters of cards from the deck, he returned to the stage and divined the cards. His procedure was to ask the spectator to fan his cards and concentrate upon them. "You are now looking at a five spot," Joseffy would say. "You are looking at the five of spades." The spectator was of course looking at all the cards he held and he would acknowledge any of these that the performer named. But to the audience, Joseffy was apparently identifying the particular card upon which the spectator's mind was at that moment focused. It was as persuasive a mental effect with cards as I have ever seen.

A committee of four was then invited to the stage, and I took advantage of the offer to see Balsamo at close range. A large sheet of plate glass was introduced with a thong looped through a hole in each corner. The thongs enabled the four

Joseffy, circa 1910

spectators to support the glass comfortably. The skull, realistically modeled and mounted on a small, cylindrical base, was placed in the center of the glass. Its actions included both opening the jaws and closing them with a loud click and rotating the skull from side to side, either to take in the audience as a whole

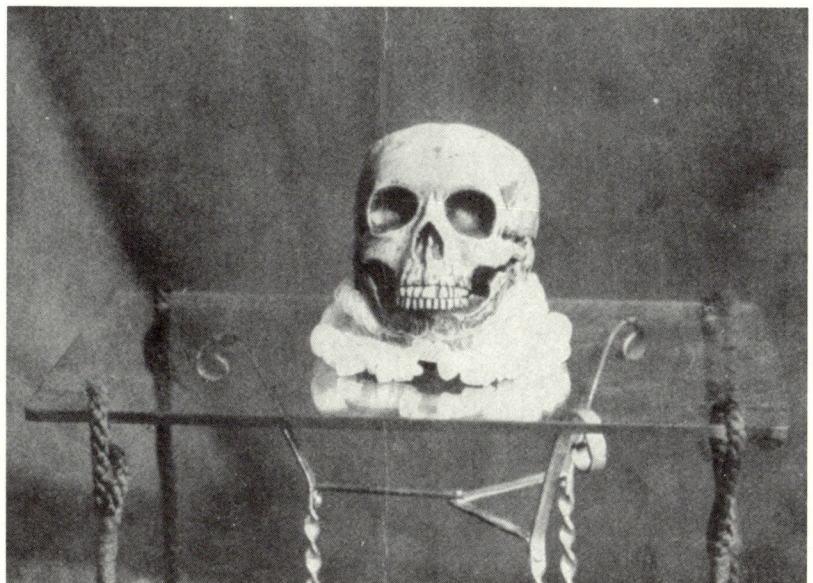

Balsamo (reproduced from The Marvelous Creations of Joseffy, *1908)*

or to fix its hollow eye sockets upon a particular spectator. Joseffy carried on a running conversation with the skull which must have consumed four or five minutes, the performer spending most of the time in the audience, asking questions, having cards taken, and so on. The instant and appropriate responses of the skull were laughable and uncanny. This illusion of communication was so complete that even though I knew this to be a timed, clockwork device, born before the age of electronic controls, I found myself looking into the wings to see if there were not someone there activating the thing through some means of remote control.

Much of Joseffy's apparatus wound up in the collection of Eugene Bernstein, a Chicago attorney and magic enthusiast. For years Gene tried to construct a routine to go with the actions of the skull, but the complexity of its actions, combined with the problems of timing over a sustained period, defied his ingenuity. He brought it down to a magic club meeting one night, wound it up and let it click away. It didn't even look like Balsamo, the alter ego of Joseffy, dominating an auditorium full of people. It was just a mechanical curiosity.

Paul Rosini

In 1936, Paul Rosini (1902-1948) began an engagement which ran for 28 weeks in the Empire Room of the Palmer House in Chicago, establishing him as one of the most successful acts ever to play this famous room. Unlike other leading acts of the day, Rosini did not come to the night club field from a successful background in vaudeville. Although he had worked as an assistant to Carl Rosini, the illusionist, and Zancig, the mentalist, his idol as a performer was the intimate entertainer Max Malini. Paul Rosini's accomplishment was to take the classical repertoire of parlor magic into the cabaret.

In presentation, Rosini assumed a Continental manner natural to his heritage (he was born in Trieste) and played this role with impudent humor. He was a master of sleight of hand, of misdirection, and of effective buildup. He could hold a night club audience in breathless expectation, awaiting the turning over of a card.

Rosini's repertoire was large, enabling him to vary his act continually. A typical program was as follows:

1. *The Egg Bag.* Charmingly done, with Rosini pretending to see the egg in the air, catching it in the bag with the aid of "a tiny little waltz" from the orchestra, and the sucker effect handled very slyly.

Paul Rosini

2. *Card in Cigarette*. The torn pieces of the card were wrapped in a slip of paper, which was tossed on the floor. After the card was extracted from the cigarette and the missing corner fitted, the discarded paper package was noted as an afterthought. Rosini picked it up from the floor and poured a stream of tobacco from it.

3. *Everywhere and Nowhere*. The Hofzinser plot masterfully presented, causing laughter and utter amazement.

4. *The Thumb Tie,* expertly performed, bringing the act to a strong conclusion.

5. *Coin Routine (presented as an encore).* Five coins were caused to pass one at a time into a glass. The last coin was apparently placed on top of the head. Rosini tilted his head and the coin made its visible and audible arrival in the glass. The coins were then made to vanish one at a time, reproduced in a Coin Star, and showered into the glass.

Al Leech, the writer and card expert, learned the coin routine from Rosini, who complimented him highly on his execution of it. "Then why don't I get the kind of applause for it that you do?" Al asked. Rosini said it was a matter of dress. "For this trick, it is necessary to wear tails," he explained.

Rosini's style of performance is illustrated in a description of one of his card effects which I prepared for a memorial volume published after his death in 1948. Rosini secured the assistance of a lady and asked her to take "a tiny little peek" at one of the cards. When she did so, he said, "Did you see one? That was a stingy peek. You're sure you saw a card?" This conversation gave him ample opportunity to bring the card to the top of the deck. It also forced the assistant to fix the name of the card in her memory.

Still expressing disbelief that the lady had really seen a card (and also emphasizing the difficulty of the trick), Rosini said, "Take another peek. You're sure you see this one? Remember it." This card was also brought to the top by means of the side-steal. Rosini now announced that he would cause the card just peeked at to come to the top of the deck and built this up as a great trick. With all attention centered on the deck, he pretended to cause the miracle to take place. "Did you see me do something?" he asked the lady. She shook her head. "I did something!" Rosini told her. "What was your card?" He showed the top card, and it was the card named. There was generous applause.

At this moment when the trick seemed concluded, Rosini top-changed the card which he had just produced and threw the (changed) card face down on the table. Then, as though pleased with his success and willing to undertake something more difficult, he said, "Do you remember that first card you peeked at? What was it?" Suppose the lady said, "The Jack of Spades." Rosini said, "Say, 'Jack of Spades, come to me.'" She did. "You say that so cute, say it again," he requested. She repeated the words. Then Rosini pointed to the card lying face down on the table and said, "Show it to the people." A card trick creating more delight and amazement would be difficult to imagine.

Mysterious Smith

Albert P. (Mysterious) Smith was an outstanding showman of the 1920s and early '30s who confined his route to communities of moderate size. His procedure was to play a theater for a week, with a complete change of program during the run. His publicity feature, a coffin escape, was presented toward the end of the engagement and repeated "by popular demand," bringing a large share of his earlier audience back to the theater to see him again.

His wife's mental act was also a strong draw. In addition to her turn in the evening show, she presented ladies' matinees at which, Smith announced, "No men will be permitted in the theater—except me!" Smith apparently had just about every money-making angle covered and was said always to do good business.

The Mysterious Smith show was not gigantic in comparison with aggregations such as those of Blackstone and Dante, but it was beautifully produced and certainly *seemed* like a big show. The performance opened with the parting of successive

Mysterious Smith

travelers and the brisk entrance of the magician, whose introductory remarks concluded with the statement: "But I am going to fool you—and *how* I am going to fool you!" Then he was off and into his first effect with a little crackling laugh of fiendish delight.

Following is a Smith program as recollected from about 1932:

1. *Dancing Handkerchief.* The borrowed handkerchief performed in a slatted pen, from which it eventually jumped to the floor.

2. *Sucker Handkerchief to Egg.* (In one).

3. *Drumhead Production.* Production of large flags, concluding with France ("the land of my birth") and the U.S.A. ("the flag of my country"). Finished with livestock production.

4. *Aerial Fishing.* (In one).

5. *Vanishing Trunk.* A girl hopped into a trunk which sat on a platform. The trunk was covered with a cloth and hoisted above the stage. A second trunk was brought in and shown empty. (This was a tipover trunk with its interior painted white, which added a good deal to the convincing effect.) The cloth covering the suspended trunk dropped to the floor, the trunk was gone and the girl reappeared from the trunk just shown empty. A startling illusion very smartly presented.

6. *Pig and Bottle.* (In one). Wine was poured from a bottle and Smith and the orchestra conductor toasted each other. Calls from behind the curtain indicated that a mistake had been made. After some byplay, the bottle was broken and a guinea pig removed.

7. *Madam Olga.* Seated on a rather elaborate throne, the Madam gave impressive answers and predictions in response to questions on the minds of the audience. This was the old-style, bare-faced act in which the written questions are deposited in a

box in the lobby, and properly presented it is by far the best method. Madam Olga had an oracular delivery, ending each authoritative reading with the pronouncement, "Your QUEStion is ANswered!" Smith, meantime, moved up and down the aisles, identifying the individuals to whom her messages were addressed and urging them to "kindly CONcentrate upon the subject." All of this went on for some time to the entire satisfaction of the audience.

8. *Cut and Restored Rope.* (In one). This was the first time I had seen a Tarbell-type rope trick. When the rope which had been so clearly severed was tossed out restored, my bafflement was complete.

9. *Vanishing Phonograph.* An early Edison phonograph (the kind with a large horn) sat on a fair-sized table toward the back of the stage. The machine was wound up and played briefly, then covered with a large foulard, lifted, and carried forward. The evanishment of this ungainly object was startling to behold.

10. *Substitution Trunk.* This was performed with emphasis on speed; no spectator assistance was requested. I have since wondered why many performers spend so much time on the preliminaries of what is really more of a transformation effect than an escape mystery.

Smith retired in the mid-1930s and settled down as a photographer in a small Southern town. One summer shortly after he had disposed of his show to Howard Thurston's brother, Harry, he toured the state of Iowa with an attraction called "The White Prophet: Do the Spirits Return?" The act featured small magic and a superbly presented spirit cabinet routine employing what is generally known as the Excelsior Tie. Smith's opening address as the White Prophet was outstanding. "Ladies and gentlemen," he said, "you have come here today to learn whether the spirits return. The answer is: No, they do not."

Mysterious Smith gave his final performance in Nashville in 1942, after 48 years as a working magician. He died in St. Cloud, Florida, in 1957.

Duval

Ade Duval's "Rhapsody in Silk" was one of the few American magic acts of the period to achieve international renown. As seen at the Oriental Theatre in Chicago, about 1938, the act consisted of the 20th Century Silks, the Clay Pipes, and a gigantic silk production from a small tube.

Duval's 20th Century was outstanding in its concept and execution. Two silks were produced from the bare hands, knotted together, and rolled into a parcel which was placed on the crown of a top hat held by the girl assistant. A third silk was produced and vanished for the customary 20th Century effect. The string of silks was rolled up, another silk produced, and the effect repeated. At the finale, the tied silks were stretched between the girl and a male assistant, and another silk was produced, vanished, and caused visibly to make its reappearance in the middle of the string of silks. The various productions were beautifully handled.

The magical smoking of the clay pipes was an attractive interlude: the empty pipes were smoked bowl to bowl, then with the stems broken off, and finally the bowls were placed on a small tray, and crushed beneath the foot, with large amounts of smoke produced from the gathered fragments.

Duval's enormous production of silks and streamers from a small metal tube has been described fully in an Ireland Magic

Ade Duval, 1934

Company (now Magic Inc.) publication. As shown at this time, some small tables were brought on to receive the silks produced and, of course, provide for the various loads. Several years later, an attractive basket was substituted for this purpose. In any case, from the audience point of view, the entire act was presented on a bare stage.

In a later appearance in Chicago, Duval introduced his original version of the smoke trick, in which the only visible "apparatus" was the bare hand formed into a fist, with the thumb forming the stem of the imaginary pipe. After the death of his wife, True, Duval worked as a single and featured this trick, along with his original Silk Blowing color change routine, a version of the Sucker Die Box employing an alarm clock, and a Vanishing Cocktail Shaker.

Ade Duval (1898-1965) retired in 1955 due to illness. Before creating his silk act in 1928, he played successfully in chautauqua and lyceum.

Paul LePaul

In his introduction to *The Card Magic of LePaul,* John Mulholland wrote: "LePaul is one of the greatest manipulative magicians ever to practice the art of pleasant deception. His magic has such polish and glamour that, in describing it, all the glowing terms of the most gifted press agent rightfully may be used."

When LePaul made his first New York vaudeville appearance, in July 1928 at the Fifth Avenue Theatre, it was his immaculate attire rather than his finished manipulations that received the greatest critical praise. The theatrical magazine *Variety* commented, "LePaul, card manipulator, wears afternoon clothes with distinction and has the crispest linen in vaudeville," while *Zit's Theatrical Newspaper* wrote, "LePaul, the last word in sartorial splendor, and with face and figure to grace it, performs some card manipulations that had his audience guessing." It was apparently a very hot July in New York and, according to the clippings from Paul's notebooks, the Fifth Avenue closed for the summer the following week, going dark for the first time in 20 years. "The moral is," *Variety* said, "that vaudeville has its own problems just in the offing."

For Paul Braden, however, who had only recently adopted the stage name LePaul, this was a beginning in the big time.

Paul LePaul springing the cards into the hat

Although he had been performing professionally for nearly a decade, several important features were still to be added to his act, including the production of cards with both hands simultaneously, each hand employing a different method, which provided an applause-winning finish to his card manipulations.

Some years later, when *Variety* reviewed his act (at Loew's

LePaul early in his career

State in New York City), the verdict was much more affirmative: "Paul LePaul has come a considerable distance since his first vaude days some years ago. His patter is pointed, while the initial paper-tearing-bird-flower trick is a trim intro to his long string of card tricks. LePaul employs two boy stooges for comedy effect in selling his card transference feat. He got solid returns."

The "trim intro" consisted of tearing some pieces of tissue paper and forming them into a package from which a canary was produced. The bird, with a ribbon attached to one leg, was allowed to flutter aloft, then was gently pulled back to the performer's hands. It was placed in a small paper bag held by the girl assistant. The bag was then torn open, revealing a corsage.

A pack of cards was produced and a routine of manipulations presented, including fancy cuts and shuffles, diminishing cards, fan steals, and the spread up the arm, followed by the ribbon drop and catch. At the conclusion of this sequence, the entire pack was sprung in a long arc into the performer's top hat. This particularly showy flourish was a LePaul trademark.

There now followed a series of back and front palm manipulations and continuous production of fans of cards. LePaul was probably one of the first to use the split-fan production technique professionally, having adopted the sleight in the early 1920s on the basis, he said, of a description which he read in an English publication dated about 1916. The productions concluded with the appearance of single cards in rapid succession in both hands, the cards being thrown into a net held by the assistant.

The act concluded with the Ten Card Trick a la Leipzig, done with red and blue backed cards and utilizing an original technique. Much natural comedy was obtained with the assisting spectators. At one time LePaul also used the glass vanish under the newspaper, and may, in fact, have been the first man to use this as a stage trick. His execution of the side-steal color change was outstanding and figured importantly in his audience participation work.

In his private engagements, LePaul performed many of the card tricks described in his book, as well as such classics as Everybody's Card and the Ladies' Looking-Glass. His drawing room performances were superb.

LePaul was a finished artist who, instead of barraging his audiences with a great variety of manipulative material, selected only that which registered most strongly; he eliminated everything that was superfluous. What gave his work its extra dimension, however, was the attitude he conveyed of delight in what he did. When you come right down to it, it is a little absurd for a grown man to stand in front of a crowd flourishing playing cards. When Paul LePaul performed you were persuaded that this was the most wonderful thing a person could possibly do.

 # Who Was Rufus Steele?

I first met W. F. (Rufus) Steele in 1946 at the Chicago Magicians' Roundtable. He was then 65 years old, which seemed to me a fairly advanced age. He was a thin, dignified gentleman with a long face and the coldest grey-blue eyes I had ever seen. The habitues of the Roundtable (an informal luncheon meeting of magicians which became a Chicago institution) regarded him as a "man of mystery," primarily because he lived without visible means.

Rufus, while doing everything to encourage the legend, asserted that the facts of his life were simple and well known. He said he was born in Janesville, Wisconsin, in 1881, that he grew up in New England, and that he studied electrical engineering at Massachusetts Institute of Technology. While a student, he worked at a Boston gambling club called the True Blue, having earlier been employed to walk the dog of the club's owner, one Dave Dishler.

The world of chance and games fascinated Rufus and led, through coincidence, to his interest in magic. While viewing the checker-playing automaton at Austin and Stone's Museum on Scollay Square, he met the celebrated card manipulator, Dr. James William Elliott (1874-1920). Their acquaintance, which began over checkers, ended in Rufus's spending many hours learning card tricks.

W. F. (Rufus) Steele

Rufus told me that he had advanced rapidly in the electrical engineering profession and had taken charge of some of the largest installation projects in the country. It was such a project, he said, that brought him to Chicago. It was here, he confided to me and to a few others, that an event occurred which provided the wherewithal for his life of mystery.

This event was the death by shooting of Marshall Field,

Jr., the 37-year-old son of the pioneer Chicago merchant. The shooting was reported by the family to have taken place at the Field home on November 22, 1905. Young Field, who suffered an abdominal wound, presumably either self-inflicted or accidental, died in a Chicago hospital five days later. Police were not allowed to see the patient or to question members of the family or their employees. Persistent rumor had it that the shooting actually occurred at a notorious and elegant sporting house known as the Everleigh Club.

Rufus confirmed this theory, stating that the injured man had been carried into a nearby hotel where Rufus was employed as desk clerk. Financial arrangements were made to gain the silence of all those concerned, and that was how Rufus Steele, at the age of 24, acquired an annuity that enabled him to spend the rest of his life as a man of mystery.

The question may occur to you as it did to me: Why was a successful young engineer working as night clerk in a cheap hotel in a highly questionable area of Chicago? Rufus indicated a tragic love affair had something to do with his turning a firsthand knowledge of gambling to professional use and consorting with what he referred to as "low life." He told of following oil and gold strikes and ending up in the Yukon, where he spent a winter in a cabin with Robert W. Service and wife. "We just rolled up in furs and grunted all winter," he said. One day he asked the woman, "Why isn't your husband writing poems?" "He can't write poetry," she said. The Yukon ballads, she told him, came from someone's abandoned safety deposit box in San Francisco.

A good many of the stories Rufus told about this period of his life ended with Rufus taking leave of the situation via the window. In fact, there were times when it seemed to me that Rufus knew no other means of egress.

At one time, he told me, he was planning to marry a very respectable young woman and was visiting her parents' home when "scenes of low life" flashed into his mind, and Rufus was straightaway out the window . . . gone!

On another occasion, he was loitering in a store in an industrial town where there was a game in the back room. The phone rang and Rufus took the call. The voice on the line said, "We've got a tip U.S. Steel has an undercover man out here looking for Wobblies." Rufus said, "Thanks," and hung up. Out the window: he was the secret agent.

Another era of his life involved the running of racehorses. This was during Prohibition. One of the tricks was to run a horse at various tracks without any particularly distinguished results, then give the beast a shot of whiskey just before a race in which they wanted the horse to win. On one occasion, the man who was supposed to bring the whiskey didn't turn up. Rufus brewed some strong tea and gave it to the horse, only to see the assistant come running up with the booze. (The drugstore had been closed and the fellow had had to track the druggist down.) Rufus added the liquor to the horse's water. The horse gulped it down and broke into a monumental sweat. There was the call to the post. "Come on," said Rufus, leading the horse. "Out of the way, please! Very nervous horse. Hates people."

I said, "Did he win?"

"No," Rufus said, "he couldn't even see the other horses."

Rufus decided to quit horse racing before he got into really bad trouble, but it was the part of his life he enjoyed the most. "I'd swim a river to do it all over," he said.

Rufus wanted me to write the story of his life and I wanted to do so, but I found it impossible. Living a lonely and rootless life, he had no sense of chronology. There was no way to place many of his stories in time or link them into a meaningful sequence.

I was, however, able to write some magic books for him: *52 Amazing Card Tricks* (1949), *Paul Rosini's Magical Gems* (1950), and *The Last Word on Cards* (1952). In doing so, I discovered that Rufus was incapable of writing a grammatical sentence. This raised a question in my mind about his college education, particularly in a day when grammar was given more attention in the schools than it is today. But Rufus was certainly knowledgeable about card table artifice and he was a connoisseur of card magic. Card workers knew he appreciated their tricks and wanted to be represented in his books. Bert Allerton, Arthur Buckley, Dr. Jacob Daley, Martin Gardner, Stuart Judah, Ken Krenzel, Al Leech, Ed Marlo, Carmen D'Amico, John Scarne, Bill Simon, Dai Vernon, Audley Walsh, and Oscar Weigle were among those who contributed. Rufus and I split the profits on these books; he was straight as an arrow financially.

Rufus's great friendship with Paul Rosini is reflected in the memorial book he put together after Rosini's death. Since Rosini, although highly original in his presentation, invented few tricks, most of the "magical gems" were contributed by other magicians. Paul LePaul also respected Rufus's knowledge and indicated in his book that he learned the push-through false riffle shuffle from Rufus.

Rufus presented me with a small notebook (now in Bob Lund's American Museum of Magic) in which he had made brief notes on a vast array of card tricks, together with the names and addresses of women across the nation. He gave bridge lessons and lectures, so these could have been clients. I didn't ask. One of the addresses was that of the building in which I have lived in Chicago since 1946. "You know," Rufus said, visiting us one summer night in the late '40s, "the last time I sat on this back porch was at a party given by Mrs. Eitel." The Eitels, who owned the largest beer garden in Chicago and subsequently built the Bismarck Hotel, constructed my building in 1900.

As long as I knew him, Rufus was terribly arthritic. This did not prevent him from giving gambling lectures, which were enhanced by his dignified presentation. We once did a club show together for some West Side Elks. Without the slightest alteration in his genteel manner, Rufus concluded with one of the most coarsely physical pieces of scatological verse I have ever heard declaimed. Some of the Elks turned pale. It was a hard act to follow.

Although often in great pain, Rufus was extremely active in organized magic, serving both as president of IBM Ring 43 and as chairman of an IBM International Convention. Sometimes the vital processes would cease just about altogether and he would be carted off to the Veterans' Administration Hospital (he had served overseas in World War I and received a disability allowance). Pretty soon he would be back at the Roundtable and the magic meetings. I always felt enormous admiration for his pluck. He lived on sheer willpower, on the special power that having a secret gives you, and on those remittances. From time to time, he mentioned property in Arizona that he ought to go out and dispose of. During his last illness (he died September 9, 1955), I asked Gene Bernstein, his attorney, about this. Gene said there wasn't any property.

The question remains: Who was Rufus Steele? Was he a man who in his youth had one great brush with Fortune and lived thereafter at the soiled edges of the sporting life, passing the time in games and the congenial society of magicians? Were his stories served from a stock of Western tales and gambling lore, offered in return for a place at our family dinner table? Or was he truly a man of many affairs, who by virtue of that secret trust fund was always able to go his own way and stand once removed from the ways of others?

I, of course, am a believer in magic and in Rufus Steele . . . a man of mystery.

Index

Aerial Fishing, 37
Allerton, Bert, 50
American Museum of Magic, 50
Austin and Stone's Museum, 46
Ball Casket and Cage Canister, 26
Balsamo, 29, 30, 31, 32
Bamberg, David, 6
Bamberg, Theodore, 4-6, *16, 17,* 24
Bernstein, Eugene, 31, 51
Birch, McDonald, 23
Blackstone, Harry, Sr., 2-3, 36
Body Loads, 27
Borrowed Handkerchief in Nest of Boxes, 28
Boston, George, 2
Boughton, Harry. *See* Blackstone, Sr.
Bowl Productions, 21
Braden, Paul. *See* LePaul, Paul
Breakaway box, 23
Buckley, Arthur, 50
Burlingame, H.J., 28
Cannon, Sir Alexander, 12
Card in Cigarette, 33
Card Magic of LePaul, 41

Chicago Magicians' Roundtable, 46
Chinese Torture Cabinet, 23
Clay Pipes, 39
Coin Star, 34
Color Changes with Pack of Cards, 27
Cut and Restored Rope, 38
Cut and Restored Turban, 19-20
D'Amico, Carmen, 50
Daley, Dr. Jacob, 50
Dancing Handkerchief, 37
Dante, 36
Davidson Theatre, 2
Dove Decapitation, 27
Dove production, 22-23
Duck Vanish, 28
Duval, Ade, 39-41
Duval, True, 41
Egg Bag, 32
Elliott, Dr. James William, 46
Erlanger Theatre, 4
Everleigh Club, 48
Everybody's Card, 44
Everywhere and Nowhere, 33
Excelsior Tie, 38
Field, Marshall, 47-48

Page numbers in italics refer to photographs.

Index

Fifth Avenue Theatre, 41
Fifty-Two Amazing Card Tricks, 50
Freud, Josef. *See* Joseffy
Gardner, Martin, 50
Gwynne, Ann, 21
Gwynne, Jack, 19-22
Heany, Gerald, 1
Here's Power, 11
Hofzinser, 33
Hubbard, Elbert, 9
Ink to Water, 27
Inside Magic, 2
International Brotherhood of Magicians, 51
Ireland Magic Company, 39-40
Joseffy, 29-32
Judah, Stuart, 50
Kim. *See* Kuma
Krenzel, Ken, 50
Kuma, 23
Kuma Tubes, 23
Ladies' Looking-Glass, 44
Larsen brothers, 9
Last Word On Cards, 50
Leaves from Conjurers' Scrap Books, 28
Leech, Al, 34, 50
LePaul, Paul, 41-45, 50
Linking Rings, 17
Loew's State, 42-43
Lund, Bob, 50
Madam Olga, 37-38
Magic Castle, 9
Magic, Inc., 39-40
Malini, Max, 32
Marlo, Ed, 50
Marshall, Frances, 10

Miller, Charles Earle, 7-9
Morris, William, 9
Mulholland, John, 13-15, 41
Mysterious Smith, 35-39
Okito. *See* Bamberg, Theodore
Okito On Magic, 2, 4
Oriental Theatre, 39
Oxford Book of Literary Anecdotes, 1
Palace Theatre, Chicago, 19
Paper-tearing-bird-flower trick, 43-44
Parrish, Mary, *10*
Paul Rosini's Magical Gems, 50
Pig and Bottle, 37
Players Club, 13
Production of Bowls of Water, 27
Production of Rabbit from a Box, 19
Rapp, Gus, 16
Redpath Bureau, 25
Reno, Ed, 24-28
Richardine, Marga, 16, 17
Richardine, Ricardo, Jr., 16, 17
Richardine, Ricardo, Sr., 15-18
Ring in the Nest of Boxes, 15
Rising Cards, 27
Rolle, John B., 11
Rosini, Carl, 32-35, 50
Rosini, Paul, 32
Rooster Vanish from a Small Box, 20-21
Scala-Berlin, 6
Scarne, John, 50
Senate Theatre, *16*
Service, Robert W., 48
Silk Blowing, 41

Index

Silk production, 23, 39
Silks and Stack of Bowls Production, 21
Simon, Bill, 50
Skull of Balsamo. *See* Balsamo
Smith, Albert P. *See* Mysterious Smith
Spirit Table, 22
Steele, W. F. (Rufus), 46-52
Stowell's Oriental Oddities, 22-24
Substitution Trunk, 38
Sucker Die Box, 41
Sucker Handkerchief to Egg, 37
Sucker Torn and Restored Napkin, 26
Sword Cabinet, Doll House version, 21
Tarbell, Harlan, 9-13, 38
Temple of Benares, 21
Ten Card Trick a la Leipzig, 44
Tenkai Two-Glass Suspension, 22
The Sphinx, 13
Thumb Tie, 34
Thurston, Harry, 38
Thurston, Howard, 6, 38
Torn and Restored Magazine Page, 21-22
Twentieth Century Silks, 39
Vanishing Bowl of Water, 22
Vanishing Cane, 26
Vanishing Cocktail Shaker, 41
Vanishing Phonograph, 38
Vanishing Trunk, 37
Vanishing Wand, 26
Variety, 41, 42
Vernon, Dai, 50
Walsh, Audley, 50
Weigle, Oscar, 50
Wild Kingdom, 17
Willard Family, 16
Zancig, 6, 32
Zit's Theatrical Newspaper, 41

This monograph was designed
by Dan Franklin
and typeset by Village Typographers, Inc.
of Waterloo, Illinois.